MW00443693

Functional React

Quick start with React Hooks, Redux and MobX

Cristian Salcescu

Functional React

Functional React

Quick start with React Hooks, Redux and MobX

Cristian Salcescu

Copyright © 2019 Cristian Salcescu

ISBN-13: 978-1072614838

History:

June 2019 First Edition

Contents

8

Preface

React is one of the most popular JavaScript libraries for creating user interfaces.

The basic unit for a piece of the user interface is the component. With React Hooks we can express all the user interface using function components.

This is a book for beginners in React, but not for beginners in JavaScript. For a better understanding of JavaScript and functional programming consider reading Discover Functional JavaScript.

Through this book, we are going to build a shopping cart. We will build all components using functions. Classes will not be used to create components or any other objects. More than that, the `this` pseudo-parameter will not be used at all.

We are going to look at state management with React Hooks and with external libraries like Redux or MobX.

React embraces functional programming. Programming in a functional style means to use concepts such as pure functions, immutability, closures, higher-order components, partial application or currying. We are going to explore how to apply these functional programming techniques in React.

Mastering the fundamentals makes us better at solving more complex tasks.

Source Code

The project files from this book are available at https://github.com/cristi-salcescu/functional-react.

Feedback

I will be glad to hear your feedback. For comments, questions or suggestions regarding this book send me an email to cristi_salcescu@yahoo.com.

Fast Development Environment

The first thing we need to do, before writing any code, is to setup our development environment.

Package Manager

A package manager is a tool used to track project dependencies in an easy to use manner. At the time of writing, Node.js package manager, in short npm, is the most popular. Let's start by installing Node.js.

After the installation, the following commands can be used in command prompt to check the Node.js and npm versions:

```
node --version
npm --v
```

Create React App

The easiest way to start with a React application is to use Create React App.

To do that, run one of the following commands:

```
npm init react-app shopping-cart
```

```
npx create-react-app shopping-cart
```

npx can execute a package that wasn't previously installed.

Once the application is created the following commands can be used:

- npm start: starts the development server.

- `npm test`: starts the test runner.
- `npm run build`: builds the app for production into the `build` folder.

IDE

For code editing, we need an Integrated Development Environment, IDE in short.

My favorite is Visual Studio Code.

To start the application, first, open the application folder in Visual Studio Code. Then open the terminal from Terminal→New Terminal and run: `npm start`. This launches the development server and opens the React application in the browser.

Linting

Linting is already enabled in Create React App. To enable linting in Visual Studio Code install the ESLint extension for VSCode and create a new configuration file `.eslintrc.json`.

Below is an example of a `.eslintrc.json` file that adds a few more rules like forbidding the use of `var`:

```
{
    "extends": [
        "react-app",
        "eslint:recommended"
    ],
    "rules": {
        "no-var": "error",
        "semi": "error",
        "max-params": ["error", 4],
        "eqeqeq" : "error"
    }
}
```

Chapter 1: Function Components

React is a library for building user interfaces. The basic unit in React is the component. The page is split into small, reusable components that are then combined together to create the whole page.

The small components are easier to reason about.

Function Components

Components can be written with functions. The following **Header** component is implemented with a function that returns an HTML-like syntax called JSX.

```
import React from "react";

export default function Header() {
  return (
    <header>
    <h1>A Shopping Cart</h1>
    </header>
  );
}
```

The **Header** component can then be used in another component called **App**.

```
import React from "react";
import Header from "./Header";

export default function App() {
```

```
  return (
    <div>
      <Header />
    </div>
  );
}
```

At this point, we have established a relation between `App` and `Header`. `App` is the parent of `Header`.

Components are organized in a tree structure with a root component. In our case, the root component is `App`.

Props

Function components can take properties.

The following `ProductItem` component takes a `product` and generates the user interface for it.

```
import React from "react";

export default function ProductItem(props) {
  return (
    <div>{props.product.name}</div>
  );
}
```

Function components take a single parameter called "props" and return the user interface markup.

We can make the code cleaner by using the destructuring assignment syntax in the parameter list.

```
export default function ProductItem({product}) {
  return (
    <div>{product.name}</div>
  );
}
```

Note that `ProductItem(props)` was replaced with `ProductItem({product})`.

Props can be passed to components using JSX attributes. Below a `product` is created and passed to the `ProductItem` component:

```
import React from "react";
import Header from "./Header";
import ProductItem from "./ProductItem";

const product = {
  id: 1,
  name : "mango"
};

export default function App() {
  return (
    <div>
      <Header />
      <div>
        <ProductItem product={product}></ProductItem>
      </div>
    </div>
  );
}
```

React passes all the component attributes in the "props" object.

Entry Point

The application has a single entry point. In our case, it is the `index.js` file. This is the place where the root component `App` is rendered. When the root component is rendered, all the other components are rendered.

```
import React from "react";
import ReactDOM from "react-dom";
import App from "./App";

ReactDOM.render(<App />, document.getElementById("root"));
```

Rendering Elements

`ReactDOM.render()` renders the component inside the root DOM element specified. Usually, there is a single root DOM element.

```
<div id="root"></div>
```

The Document Object Model, DOM, is an in-memory object representation of the HTML document. The DOM offers an application programming interface, API, that allows to read and manipulate the page's content, structure, styles and handle HTML events. The DOM is a tree-like structure.

DOM updates are expensive.

The Virtual DOM is an in-memory representation of the user interface. It is used by the React diff algorithm to identify only the necessary changes for updating the "real" DOM.

Final Thoughts

In React, we can decompose the page into small functions, rendering parts of the user interface, and then combined them to form the whole page.

Function components take in props and return the user interface markup using the JSX syntax.

Function components transform data into a visual user interface.

Chapter 2: A Brief Introduction to JSX

JSX describes how the user interface looks like. It offers a friendly HTML-like syntax for creating DOM elements.

JSX stands for JavaScript XML.

Transpiling

The JSX code is transpiled to JavaScript. See the code below:

```
//JSX
ReactDOM.render(
  <header>
      <h1>A Shopping Cart</h1>
  </header>,
  document.getElementById("root")
)
```

```
//Transpiled to JavaScript
ReactDOM.render(
  React.createElement("header", null,
    React.createElement("h1", null, "A Shopping Cart")
  ),
  document.getElementById("root")
);
```

As you can see, JSX is transpiled to `React.createElement()` calls, which create "React elements". React elements are plain objects. React uses these elements to update the DOM.

Expressions

JSX accepts any valid JavaScript expression inside curly braces.

Here are some examples of expressions:

```
function Message(){
  const message = "1+1=2";
  return <div>{message}</div>
}

function Message(){
  return <div>1+1={1+1}</div>
}

function Message(){
  const sum = (a, b) => a + b;
  return <div>1+1={sum(1, 1)}</div>
}
```

```
ReactDOM.render(<Message/>, document.querySelector("#root"));
```

An expression is a valid unit of code that resolves to a value.

For example, the conditional ternary operator is an expression, but the if statement is not.

```
function Valid({valid}){
  return <span>{ valid ? "Valid" : "Invalid"}</span>
}
```

```
ReactDOM.render(<Valid valid={false} />,
 document.getElementById("root"));
```

```
//<span>Invalid</span>
```

JSX is also an expression. It can be used inside statements, assigned to variables, passed as arguments.

Here is the previous component rewritten with JSX inside the if statement:

```
function Valid({valid}){
  if(valid){
    return <span>Valid</span>
```

```
  } else {
    return <span>Invalid</span>
  }
}
```

```
ReactDOM.render(<Valid valid={false}/>,
 document.querySelector("#root"));
```

Below is the same logic implemented by assigning JSX to a variable:

```
function Valid({valid}){
  let resultJSX;
  if(valid){
    resultJSX = <span>Valid</span>;
  } else {
    resultJSX = <span>Invalid</span>;
  }

  return resultJSX;
}
```

```
ReactDOM.render(<Valid valid={false}/>,
 document.querySelector("#root"));
```

Escaping string expressions

JSX does automatic escaping of string expressions.

```
function Message(){
  const messageText = "<b>learn</b>";
  return <span>{messageText}</span>;
}
```

```
ReactDOM.render(<Message />,
  document.querySelector("#root"));
```

The text inside `messageText` is escaped, so `<b>learn</b>` will be displayed as a text.

Below the previous code is rewritten with JSX instead of a string.

```
function Message(){
  const messageJSX = <b>learn</b>;
  return <span>{messageJSX}</span>;
```

```
}
```

```
ReactDOM.render(<Message />,
  document.querySelector("#root"));
```

This time, the "learn" text is displayed in bold.

Syntax

Function components can return a single tag. When we want to return multiple tags we need to wrap them into a new tag.

All tags need to be closed. For example, `<br>` must be written as `<br />`.

Since JSX is transpiled into `React.createElement()` calls, the React library must be available when using JSX.

```
import React from "react";
```

Components must start with a capital letter. The following code doesn't work correctly:

```
function product(){
  return <div>A product</div>
}
```

```
ReactDOM.render(<product />, document.querySelector("#root"));
```

In JSX, lower-case tag names are considered to be HTML tags, not React components.

The automatic semi-colon insertion may create problems when using `return`. The following function component will not return a React element, but `undefined`.

```
function Product(){
  return
    <div>
      A product
    </div>
}
```

A common practice, to avoid this problem, is to open parentheses on the same line as `return`.

```
function Product(){
```

```
  return (
    <div>
      A product
    </div>
  );
}
```

Attributes

The attributes in JSX use camelCase. For example `tabindex` becomes `tabIndex`, `onclick` becomes `onClick`.

Other attributes have different names than in HTML: `class` becomes `className`, `for` becomes `htmlFor`.

Consider the `Valid` component:

```
function Valid({valid}){
  return <span>{ valid ? "Valid" : "Invalid"}</span>
}
```

Curly braces can be used to specify an expression in an attribute:

```
<Valid valid={false}/>
```

In this case, the `valid` property of the props object gets the value `false`.

Quotes can be used to specify a string literal in an attribute:

```
<Valid valid="false" />
```

In this case, the `valid` property gets the string `"false"`.

Consider the next example:

```
<Valid valid="{false}" />
```

In this case, the `valid` property gets the string `"{false}"`

For attributes, we should use quotes to assign string values or curly braces to assign expressions, but not both.

Final Thoughts

JSX allows using markup directly in JS. In a sense, JSX is a mix of JS and HTML.

JSX is transpiled to `React.createElement()` calls, which create React elements.

JSX accepts expression inside curly braces. String expressions are escaped.

Attributes in JSX use camelCase.

Chapter 3: List Components

A function component transforms a value into a React element.

The `map()` method transforms a list of values into another list of values.

A list component transforms a list of values into a React element containing a list of React elements.

Let's see how.

ProductList Component

The `ProductItem` component creates the interface for a single product.

The `ProductList` component creates the interface for a list of products using `map()` and the `ProductItem` component.

```
import React from "react";
import ProductItem from "./ProductItem";

function renderProductItem(product) {
  return (
    <ProductItem
      product={product}
      key={product.id}
    />
  );
}

export default function ProductList({products}) {
  return (
```

```
    <div>
      {products.map(renderProductItem)}
    </div>
  );
}
```

`renderProductItem()` renders one product using the `ProductItem` component.

`products.map(renderProductItem)` transforms the list of products into a visual representation of `ProductItem` components.

Key

React requires to uniquely identify each item in a list. In most cases we are going to use ids as keys. Note the use of `product.id` as key to each `ProductItem`:

```
<ProductItem product={product} key={product.id} />
```

App Component

The `App` root component takes a list of `products` and sends it to the `ProductList` component.

```
import React from 'react';

import Header from './Header';
import ProductList from './ProductList';

export default function App({products}) {
  return (
    <div>
      <Header />
      <div>
        <ProductList products={products}></ProductList>
      </div>
    </div>
  );
}
```

Entry Point

The entry point file index.js creates an array of products and sends it to the App component.

```
import React from 'react';
import ReactDOM from 'react-dom';
import App from './App';

const products = [
  {
    "id" : 1,
    "name" : "mango",
    "price" : 10
  },
  {
    "id" : 2,
    "name" : "apple",
    "price": 5
  }];

ReactDOM.render(<App products={products} />,
  document.getElementById('root'));
```

Final Thoughts

A list component transforms a list of values into a visual representation of that list. map() is used for the transformation.

It is a good practice to have a component that renders a single element in the list.

Chapter 4: Communication between Components

Splitting the page into small components makes things easier to manage and reuse, but it creates a new challenge, the communication between these components.

React events are handled similar to DOM events.

The attributes for React events are named using camelCase. `onClick`, `onChange`, `onSubmit` are examples of attributes for event handling.

The callback functions for handling events are passed inside curly braces.

Events with props

ProductItem Component

Let's take the case of adding a product to the cart.

The `ProductItem` component takes a `product` object to display and the `onAddClick()` callback to be called on the Add click.

```
export default function ProductItem({product, onAddClick}) {}
```

When the Add button is clicked we need to execute the callback with the current product as an argument. One way to do it is to create an anonymous function that executes the callback with the `product` argument.

```
onClick={() => onAddClick(product)}
```

Another option is to use partial application for passing arguments to event handlers.

Partial application is the process of fixing a number of arguments to a function by producing another function with fewer
arguments.

With the `partial()` utility function we can create an event handler with
the `product` argument already applied.

```
import partial from "lodash/partial";
```

```
onClick={partial(onAddClick, product)}
```

Here is the full `ProductItem` component:

```
import React from "react";
import partial from "lodash/partial";

export default function ProductItem({product, onAddClick}) {
  return (
    <div>
      <div>{product.name}</div>
      <div>
      <button type="button"
        onClick={partial(onAddClick, product)}>
       Add
      </button>
      </div>
    </div>
  );
}
```

`ProductItem` exposes the `onAddClick` event as a property. The parent
component should pass a callback to handle the event. The callback will
be called when the Add button is clicked.

Child components communicate with their parents using callbacks. Parent
components set the callbacks using attributes.

ProductList Component

`ProductList` exposes also the `onAddClick` event as a property. It
does nothing more than assigning the `onAddClick()` callback to the
`onAddClick` event.

```
import React from "react";
```

```
import ProductItem from "./ProductItem";

export default function ProductList({products, onAddClick}){
  function renderProductItem(product) {
    return (
      <ProductItem
        product={product}
        key={product.id}
        onAddClick={onAddClick}
      />
    );
  }

  return (
    <div>
      {products.map(renderProductItem)}
    </div>
  );
}
```

Handling Events

App handles the onAddClick event by writing the product to console.

```
import React from 'react';

import Header from './Header';
import ProductList from './ProductList';

export default function App({products}) {
  function addToCart(product) {
    console.log(product);
  }

  return (
    <div>
      <Header />
      <div>
        <ProductList products={products}
          onAddClick={addToCart}>
        </ProductList>
```

```
      </div>
    </div>
  );
}
```

Data Flow

Let's see how data flows between components.

The entry point creates the `products` and passes them to `App`. From there, `App` sends them to `ProductList`. Then `ProductList` passes each `product` to the `ProductItem` components.

Data flow with props: Entry point → `App` → `ProductList` → `ProductItem`.

When the Add button is clicked in `ProductItem`, it calls the `onAddClick()` provided by `ProductList`, which calls the `onAddClick()` callback provided by `App`. In a sense, data travels from children to parents using callbacks.

Data flow with callbacks: `ProductItem` → `ProductList` → `App`.

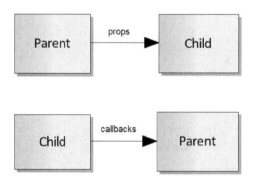

Final Thoughts

Parent components send data to child components using props.

On user interactions, child components invoke the callbacks provided by the parent components with new data.

Chapter 5: Presentation Components

Presentation components transform data into a visual representation.

Presentation components communicate only through their own props.

Let's build the ShoppingItem and ShoppingCart presentation components.

ShoppingItem Component

ShoppingItem gets a product and creates the JSX markup for one item in the shopping cart.

It takes a callback to handle the onClick event.

```
import React from "react";
import partial from "lodash/partial";

export default function ShoppingItem({product,onRemoveClick}){
  return (
    <div>
        <div>{product.name}</div>
        <div>{product.quantity}</div>
        <div>
          <button type="button"
          onClick={partial(onRemoveClick, product)}>
          Remove
          </button>
        </div>
    </div>
```

```
  );
}
```

ShoppingList Component

ShoppingList gets a cart object and creates the JSX markup for it.

ShoppingList takes the onRemoveClick() callback and assigns it to the onRemoveClick event.

```
import React from "react";
import ShoppingItem from "./ShoppingItem";

export default function ShoppingCart({cart, onRemoveClick}) {
  function renderShoppingItem(product) {
    return (
      <ShoppingItem
        product={product}
        key={product.id}
        onRemoveClick={onRemoveClick}
      />
    );
  }

  return (
    <div>
      <div>
        {cart.list.map(renderShoppingItem)}
      </div>
      <div>Total: {cart.total}</div>
    </div>
  );
}
```

Pure Functions

A pure function is a function that given the same input always returns the same output and has no side effects.

Pure functions make code easier to read and understand.

Changing the outside environment in any way is a side effect. Reading a variable from the outside environment that can change is a side effect.

All the components we have built so far `ProductItem`, `ProductList`, `ShoppingList`, `ShoppingItem`, `App` are presentation components. More than that, they are pure functions.

`ShoppingItem` is a pure function no matter if the `onRemoveClick()` callback is pure or impure. Note that `ShoppingItem` doesn't execute the `onRemoveClick()`. It creates a new function with the `product` already applied as the first argument and assigns it to the event.

Writing components as pure functions makes the code easier to reason about.

Props

Presentation components take two kinds of inputs, plain data objects and callbacks.

The plain objects are the data to be transformed into a user interface.

The callbacks are used to communicate user interactions.

Final Thoughts

Presentation components transform data into a visual interface.

Presentation components are best implemented as pure functions.

Chapter 6: Styling Components

Before going further, let's apply some styling to existing components.

A few CSS concepts

Visual HTML elements can be split into two, inline and block elements.

Block vs inline

Block level elements include tags like `div`, `header`, `footer`. They act as containers for other inline or block elements. A block element starts on a new line and extends to the width of its parent. It can be sized using `width` and `height`.

Inline elements include tags like `span` , `input`, `select`. They have the `width` and `height` of their content. Inline elements are displayed on the same line unless there is not enough space on that line. Inline elements can't be sized using `width` and `height`.

Normal Document Flow

The normal document flow is the default way for displaying elements on a page. Block elements are put on new rows from top to bottom and inline element are displayed one after the other, from left to right.

The Box Model

At the core of the page layout is the box model. Any visible HTML element is considered to be in a rectangular box defined by content (`width`, `height`), `padding`, `border`, and `margin`.

Selectors

Selectors select elements on the page. The most common are:

- The id selector `#id` selects an element with a specific id attribute. The id of an element should be unique in the page.
- The class selector `.className` selects all elements with a specific `class` attribute.
- The tag selector `tagName` selects all elements based on their tag name.

CSS Syntax

A CSS rule consists of a selector and a set of CSS properties. Each property has a name and a value.

The next rule selects the `header` tag and sets the `text-align` property to `center`.

```
header {
    text-align: center;
}
```

Flex Layout

`display: flex` defines the flex container. By default all its direct children are display from left to right on a single line.

The `flex-direction` property defines the direction in which flex items are placed in the flex container. The `row` value displays the flex items horizontally, from left to right and the `column` value displays the flex items vertically, from top to bottom.

Styling Components

We will define a CSS file specific for each component. The CSS file will have the same name as the JSX file.

ProductItem CSS

The `.product-list-item` class defines the style for each product item.

```
.product-list-item {
    padding: 10px;
    margin: 10px;
```

```
    background-color: #CC6500;
    color: #FFF;
}
```

Create React App uses Webpack for handling all assets, including CSS files. Webpack extends the concept of `import` beyond JavaScript. To use a CSS file inside a component, we need to import it.

Here is how we can use the `ProductItem.css` file in `ProductItem.jsx`:

```
import React from "react";
import partial from "lodash/partial";
import "./ProductItem.css";

export default function ProductItem({product, onAddClick}) {
  return (
    <div className="product-list-item">
      <div>{product.name}</div>
      <div>
        <button type="button"
          onClick={partial(onAddClick, product)}>
          Add
        </button>
      </div>
    </div>
  );
}
```

ShoppingItem CSS

The `.shopping-cart-item` class defines the style for each shopping item.

```
.shopping-cart-item {
    padding: 10px;
    margin: 10px;
    color: #FFF;
    background-color: #FF9C00;
    display: flex;
    flex-direction: column;
}

.shopping-cart-item div {
    margin: 5px;
```

```
}
```

ShoppingCart CSS

The .shopping-cart-total class defines the style for the total price.

```
.shopping-cart-total {
    padding: 10px;
    margin: 10px;
    color: #654321;
    border: 1px solid #FF9C00;
}
```

App CSS

The App.css defines the page layout and the default look for elements common to all components, like buttons.

```
button {
    background: #FAF1DD;
    border: 1px solid #FAF1DD;
    color: #654321;
    padding: 5px;
    cursor: pointer;
}

header {
    text-align: center;
}

//layout
.content {
    display: flex;
    width: 70%;
    margin: 0 auto;
}

.content > div{
    flex : 1;
}
```

Final Thoughts

CSS defines the look and feel of an HTML page.

In normal document flow block elements are displayed on new lines from top to bottom and inline elements are displayed on the same line from left to right.

Component styles can be defined in separate CSS files. Webpack allows importing CSS files inside components.

Chapter 7: State with React Hooks

Data can take two forms, props and state.

So far, we have seen pure function components that take data as props and transform it into a visual interface. In that case, data is passed from parent components to child components.

State

State is data that is stored and can change.

With React Hooks we can create function components that store state.

The `useState()` hook function can be used to add local state to a function component.

```
import React, { useState } from "react";

export default function App({products}) {
  const [shoppingMap, setShoppingMap] =
    useState(Object.create(null));

  //...
}
```

`useState()` returns a variable holding the current state and a function to update it. `useState()` takes an argument as the initial state value. Changing state triggers a re-render.

The `App` component will store a map with all products added to the shopping cart and their quantity.

A map is a dynamic collection of key-value pairs. `Object.create(null)` creates an empty map.

`shoppingMap` gets the current map. `setShoppingMap()` updates the map and re-renders the component.

Here is the implementation of the `App` component:

```
import React from "react";
import { useState } from "react";
import partial from "lodash/partial";
import "./App.css";

import Header from "./Header";
import ShoppingCart from "./ShoppingCart";
import ProductList from "./ProductList";

export default function App({products}) {
  const [shoppingMap, setShoppingMap] =
    useState(Object.create(null));

  function addToCart(product) {
    const addToMap = partial(addProductToMap, product);
    setShoppingMap(addToMap);
  }

  function removeFromCart(product) {
    const removeFromMap = partial(removeProductFromMap,product);
    setShoppingMap(removeFromMap);
  }

  return (
    <div>
      <Header />
      <div className="content">
        <ProductList products={products}
         onAddClick={addToCart}>
        </ProductList>
        <ShoppingCart cart={toCartView(shoppingMap)}
         onRemoveClick={removeFromCart}>
        </ShoppingCart>
      </div>
```

```
      </div>
   );
}
```

addToCart() handles the Add click by adding the new product to the map.

removeFromCart() handles the Remove click by removing the product from the map.

setShoppingMap() can take a mapping function as an argument. The mapping function takes the previous state value and returns the new state value.

Pure Functions

All state modifications are made using pure functions.

addProductToMap() takes a product and a map and returns the new map with the product quantity updated.

```
function addProductToMap(product, shoppingMap){
   const newShoppingMap = { ...shoppingMap };
   newShoppingMap[product.id] =
      incrementProductQuantity(product, shoppingMap);
   return Object.freeze(newShoppingMap);
}
```

Pure functions don't modify their input values. For this reason, the shoppingMap is first cloned. The spread operator is used to create a shallow copy of the input map: { ...shoppingMap }.

> Object.freeze() freezes an object. A frozen object cannot be changed.

deleteProductFromMap() takes a product and a map and returns the new map with the product removed.

```
function removeProductFromMap(product, shoppingMap){
   const newShoppingMap = { ...shoppingMap };
   delete newShoppingMap[product.id];
   return Object.freeze(newShoppingMap);
}
```

incrementProductQuantity() takes a product and a map and returns a new product with the quantity updated

```
function incrementProductQuantity(product, shoppingMap) {
  const quantity =
    getProductQuantity(product, shoppingMap) + 1;
  return Object.freeze({ ...product, quantity });
}
```

getProductQuantity() takes a product and a map and returns the current quantity of that product.

```
function getProductQuantity(product, shoppingMap) {
  const existingProduct = shoppingMap[product.id];
  if (existingProduct) {
    return existingProduct.quantity;
  }

  return 0;
}
```

toCartView() converts a map to a list of products plus the total price. The the total price is computed using the addPrice() reducer function.

```
function toCartView(shoppingMap) {
  const shoppingList = Object.values(shoppingMap);
  return Object.freeze({
    list: shoppingList,
    total: shoppingList.reduce(addPrice, 0)
  });
}
```

```
function addPrice(totalPrice, line) {
  return totalPrice + line.price * line.quantity;
}
```

The pure functions can be extracted out from the component and then exported to be tested.

At this point, all the logic managing the state is inside the **App** root component. All the other components are presentation components taking data as props.

Final Thoughts

Data has two forms, props and state.

The `useState()` hook defines state inside a function component.

State transformations can be done with pure functions taking the previous state as a parameter and returning the new state.

Chapter 8: State with Custom Store

Let's extract all the state management code out of the `App.js` file.

We will create a new store object responsible for managing the shopping cart.

Event Emitter

The store object emits events. For this task, we will use a micro event emitter.

```
npm install micro-emitter --save
```

The emitter object is used to emit and register event handlers.

```
const eventEmitter = new MicroEmitter();
const CHANGE_EVENT = "change";

//emit event
eventEmitter.emit(CHANGE_EVENT);

//register event handlers
eventEmitter.on(CHANGE_EVENT, handler);
```

Store

The main purpose of the `ShoppingCartStore` is to store and manage the current shopping cart.

The store emits events every time its state changes. Components can subscribe to these events and update the user interface.

The `ShoppingCartStore` is the single source of truth regarding the shopping cart.

Consider the following implementation of the store:

```
import MicroEmitter from "micro-emitter";

//pure functions

export default function ShoppingCartStore() {
  const eventEmitter = new MicroEmitter();
  const CHANGE_EVENT = "change";

  let shoppingMap = new Map();

  function addToCart(product) {
    shoppingMap = addProductToMap(product, shoppingMap);
    eventEmitter.emit(CHANGE_EVENT);
  }

  function removeFromCart(product) {
    shoppingMap = removeProductFromMap(product, shoppingMap);
    eventEmitter.emit(CHANGE_EVENT);
  }

  function get() {
    return toCartView(shoppingMap);
  }

  function onChange(handler) {
    eventEmitter.on(CHANGE_EVENT, handler);
  }

  function offChange() {
    eventEmitter.off(CHANGE_EVENT);
  }

  return Object.freeze({
    addToCart,
    removeFromCart,
    get,
```

```
  onChange,
  offChange
});
}
```

The `ShoppingCartStore()` is a factory function. It builds encapsulated objects. The `shoppingMap` is hidden. Factory functions don't use the confusing `this` pseudo-parameter.

Entry Point

The store needs to be created and sent to components.

`index.js` is the application entry point. This is the place where the store is created. It is then sent to the `App` component using props.

```
import ShoppingCartStore from "./ShoppingCartStore";

const shoppingCartStore = ShoppingCartStore();

ReactDOM.render(<App products={products}
   shoppingCartStore={shoppingCartStore} />,
   document.getElementById('root'));
```

Using the Store

The `App` root component communicates with the store.

React is a data-driven UI library. We need to update the data in order to modify the user interface. We can use the `useState()` hook function to define the `cart` object that is updated when the store changes. `setCart()` updates the `cart`.

When the store emits a change event, the component changes the local state and the UI is re-rendered.

```
import React from "react";
import { useState, useEffect } from "react";
import "./App.css";
import ShoppingCart from "./ShoppingCart";

import Header from "./Header";
import ProductList from "./ProductList";
```

```
export default function App({products, shoppingCartStore}) {
  const [cart, setCart] = useState({list: []});

  useEffect(subscribeToStore, []);

  function subscribeToStore() {
    shoppingCartStore.onChange(reload);

    return function cleanup(){
      shoppingCartStore.offChange();
    };
  }

  function reload() {
    const cart = shoppingCartStore.get();
    setCart(cart);
  }

  return (
    <div>
      <Header />
      <div className="content">
        <ProductList products={products}
          onAddClick={shoppingCartStore.addToCart}>
        </ProductList>
        <ShoppingCart cart={cart}
          onRemoveClick={shoppingCartStore.removeFromCart}>
        </ShoppingCart>
      </div>
    </div>
  );
}
```

Effect Hook

The effect hook performs side effects in function components. Any communication with the outside environment is a side effect.

The "effect" is a function that runs after React performs the DOM updates. The effect function has access to the state variables.

The effect function runs after every render.

`useEffect()` can skip running an effect if specific values haven't changed between re-renders. For this, we need to pass an array as an optional second argument to the function. React compares the values in the array from the previous render with the values in the array from the next render and when all items in the array are the same React skips running the effect.

When we want to run the effect only once, we pass an empty array (`[]`) as a second argument. In this case, the props and state inside the effect function have their initial values.

The following code runs the effect only once. It subscribes to store events only once.

```
useEffect(loadAndSubscribe, []);

function loadAndSubscribe() {
  shoppingCartStore.onChange(reload);
}
```

Effects with Cleanup

The effect is a function. If this function returns another function, the returned function is then run to clean up.

The cleanup function is the return function from an effect.

When effects run more than once, React cleans up the effects from the previous render before running the next effects.

```
useEffect(subscribeToStore, []);

function subscribeToStore() {
  shoppingCartStore.onChange(reload);
  return function cleanup(){
    shoppingCartStore.offChange();
  };
}
```

Final Thoughts

Stores offer a way to encapsulate state and share the state management behavior between components.

A store object emits events when its state changes.

The effect hook allows having side effects inside components.

Chapter 9: State with MobX

MobX allows creating stores with observable state.

To install MobX, run the following commands:

```
npm install mobx --save
npm install mobx-react --save
```

Store

With MobX we can create the state in `ShoppingCartStore` as an observable map.

```
import { observable, action } from "mobx";

//pure functions

export default function ShoppingCartStore(){
  const shoppingMap = observable.map();

  function toCartView() {
    return toCartViewFromMap(shoppingMap);
  }

  //actions
  const addToCart = action(function(product){
    shoppingMap.set(product.id,
      incrementProductQuantity(shoppingMap, product));
  });
```

```
const removeFromCart = action(function(product){
  shoppingMap.delete(product.id);
});

return Object.freeze({
  addToCart,
  removeFromCart,
  toCartView
});
}
```

observable.map() defines an observable map.

The observable() function makes objects and arrays observable.

Once state is observable, we can turn components into observers and react to changes by re-rendering.

In MobX actions are functions that modify the state. Action functions should be marked using the action() decorator. This will make sure that intermediate changes are not visible until the action has finished.

The ShoppingCartStore defines two actions for adding and removing products from the cart and exposes them as public methods. It also makes public the method for getting the current cart.

Container Components

Presentation components don't communicate with the outside environment using a publish-subscribe pattern. The ShoppingCartStore can't be used in presentation components.

We want to keep presentation components as pure functions and get all the benefits of purity. We can use container components to connect stores to presentation components.

Container components provide data to presentation components and define handlers for events in presentation components. Container components may be impure, they may call methods on stores for example.

ProductList Container

The `ProductList` presentation component is a pure function. We will create a container that makes the connection between the presentation component and the store.

`inject()` can be used to get access to the MobX store.

> `inject()` creates a higher-order component that makes the stores available to the wrapped component. `inject()` can take a mapper function. The mapper function receives all stores as an argument and creates the object mapping properties to data and callbacks.

> A higher-order component is a function that takes a component and returns a new component.

Here is the container component that handles the `onAddClick` event.

```
import { inject } from "mobx-react";

import ProductList from '../ProductList';

const withPropsMapped = inject(function(stores){
  return {
    onAddClick : stores.shoppingStore.addToCart
  };
});

export default withPropsMapped(ProductList);
```

ShoppingCart Container

Once the store is observable we can make the `ShoppingCart` component an observer. It means that when the state changes inside the store the `ShoppingCart` component will re-render.

> `observer()` takes a component an creates a new one that will re-render when state changes. Components become reactive.

```
import { inject, observer } from "mobx-react";

import ShoppingCart from "../ShoppingCart";
```

```
const withPropsMapped = inject(function(stores){
  return {
    cart : stores.shoppingStore.toCartView(),
    onRemoveClick: stores.shoppingStore.removeFromCart
  };
});

export default withPropsMapped(observer(ShoppingCart));
```

Entry Point

The index.js is the application single entry point. Here is where the store is created.

We can send the store down to components using props, but a simpler way is to use the React Context. React Context can be used to share data that is considered to be "global".

The Provider component from the mobx-react package can be used to send the stores down to components. Provider uses the React Context. The root component App should be wrapped inside the Provider component.

```
import React from "react";
import ReactDOM from "react-dom";
import App from "./App";
import { Provider } from "mobx-react";
import ShoppingCartStore from "./stores/ShoppingCartStore";

const products = [
    //...
    ];

const shoppingStore = ShoppingCartStore();

ReactDOM.render(<Provider shoppingStore={shoppingStore}>
  <App products={products} />
  </Provider>,
  document.getElementById("root"));
```

Final Thoughts

MobX allows to defined observable state.

`observer()` turns components into reactive components. The observer components re-render when the state changes.

Container components can connect presentation components to stores.

Chapter 10: State with Redux

Redux does state management using functional principles.

To start using the Redux store, install the following packages:

```
npm install redux --save
npm install react-redux --save
```

Store

In Redux there is a single store that manages all the application state tree.

The store has the `getState()` method that gets all state as a read-only immutable value.

The store in Redux is a dispatcher. It has a `dispatch()` method. The state inside the store can be changed only by dispatching actions. There are no state setters on the store object.

Reducers

The Redux store manages state using pure functions called reducers. These functions take the previous state and an action as parameters and return the new state.

The store applies reducers when an action is dispatched.

The Redux store does state changes, but these changes are encapsulated behind the library. We write only the pure functions and let the library apply them and do the state modifications.

Let's write the reducer for managing the shopping cart.

```
import { Map } from "immutable";

export default function shoppingCart(shoppingMap=Map(),action){
  switch (action.type) {
    case "add_to_cart":
      return addToCart(shoppingMap, action.product);
    case "remove_from_cart":
      return removeFromCart(shoppingMap, action.product);
    default:
      return shoppingMap;
  }
}

function addToCart(shoppingMap, product) {
  const newProduct =
    incrementProductQuantity(shoppingMap, product);
  return shoppingMap.set(product.id, newProduct);
}

function removeFromCart(shoppingMap, product) {
  return shoppingMap.remove(product.id);
}

function incrementProductQuantity(shoppingMap, product) {
  const quantity =
    getProductQuantity(shoppingMap, product) + 1;
  return Object.freeze({ ...product, quantity });
}

function getProductQuantity(shoppingMap, product) {
  const existingProduct = shoppingMap.get(product.id);
  if (existingProduct) {
    return existingProduct.quantity;
  }

  return 0;
}
```

The state is initialized with an empty immutable map.

When the "add_to_cart" action is dispatched, the state changes to a new map with the quantity for the specified product updated. The product is found in action.product.

When the "remove_from_cart" action is dispatched, the state changes to a new map with the product removed. The product to delete is taken from action.product.

Reducers are used to change state, not to get the state from the store.

Root Reducer

Redux requires one root reducer. We can create many reducers managing parts of the root state and then combine them together with combineReducers() and create the root reducer.

```
import { combineReducers } from "redux";
import shoppingCart from "./shoppingCart";

export default combineReducers({
  shoppingCart
});
```

Here is how the flow inside the store looks like:

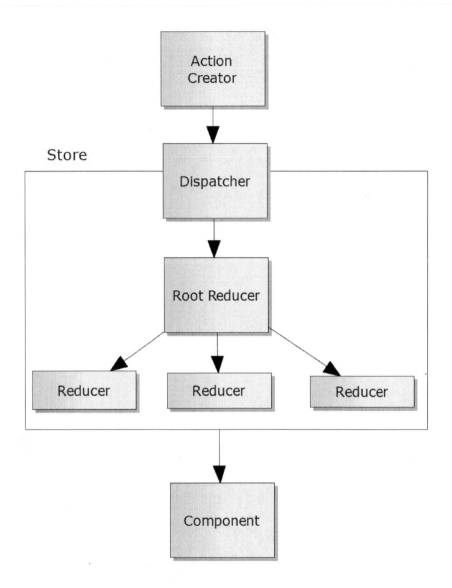

Immutability

An immutable value is a value that, once created, cannot be changed.

The state value is immutable, so each time we want to change the state we need to create a new immutable value.

The state can change but its value is immutable. There is no point to use a library to manage state that doesn't change.

Immutable.js provides immutable data structures like `Map` and `List`. To install the library run the following command:

```
npm install immutable --save
```

Let's take a look at Map.

`Map()` creates a immutable map. `Map` is a factory function, it does not use the `new` keyword.

```
let shoppingMap = Map()
```

> `set(key, value)` returns a new Map containing the new key-value pair.

> `remove(key)` returns a new Map without the specified key.

Entry Point

We create the store in the application entry point, the `index.js`.

We can use the `Provider` component from the `react-redux` to send the store down to components. To send the store to all components we wrap the root component inside the `Provider`. The store is then available to components using the `connect()` function.

```
import React from 'react';
import ReactDOM from 'react-dom';
import { createStore } from "redux";
import { Provider } from "react-redux";

import App from './App';
import rootReducer from "./reducers";

const products = [
    //...
    ];

const store = createStore(rootReducer);

ReactDOM.render(<Provider store={store}>
  <App products={products} /></Provider>,
  document.getElementById('root'));
```

Actions

Actions are plain data objects containing all the necessary information to make an action.

Let's imagine what are the necessary information for adding a product to cart. First the application needs to know that it is an "add_to_cart" action, second it needs to know the product to be added to the cart. Here is how the "add_to_cart" action may look like:

```
{
  type: "add_to_cart",
  product
}
```

The action object needs the type property indicating the action to perform. type is usually a string.

Action objects should be treated as immutable.

Action Creators

A common practice is to encapsulate the code that creates the plain action objects in functions. These functions are pure functions called action creators.

```
function addToCart(product) {
  return {
    type: "add_to_cart",
    product
  };
}

function removeFromCart(product) {
  return {
    type: "remove_from_cart",
    product
  };
}

export { addToCart, removeFromCart };
```

Presentation Components

We will use the same presentation components.

Presentation components communicate only through their own props. They don't have access to the store object.

Container Components

The `ProductList` is a presentation component that requires the list of `products` in order to render the user interface.

We need a way to take the data from the store, process it and send it to the `ProductList` component. This is the role of the container component.

For this, we will use the `connect()` higher order component from `redux-connect` package.

> `connect()` connects a component to a Redux store.

The container component does the following:

- It takes the state from the store, processes it with a selector and then sends the result to the presentation component as props. The `mapStateToProps()` does that.
- It defines the actions to be dispatched when events are triggered by the user interaction. The `mapDispatchToProps()` does that.

ProductList Container

The `ProductListContainer` component dispatches the `"add_to_cart"` action on the `onAddClick` event.

```
import { connect } from "react-redux";
import { addToCart } from "../actions/ShoppingCartActions";
import ProductList from "../ProductList";

function mapStateToProps(state) {
  return {};
}

function mapDispatchToProps(dispatch) {
  return {
    onAddClick: function(product){
      dispatch(addToCart(product));
```

```
    }
  };
}


export default connect(
  mapStateToProps,
  mapDispatchToProps
)(ProductList);
```

ShoppingCart Container

The ShoppingCartContainer connects the ShoppingCart component to
the store. It reads state from the store, transforms it and sends it to the
presentation component. On the onRemoveClick event, it dispatches the
"remove_from_cart" action.

```
import { connect } from "react-redux";
import { removeFromCart } from "../actions/ShoppingCartActions";
import { toCartView } from "../reducers/shoppingCart";
import ShoppingCart from "../ShoppingCart";

function mapStateToProps(state) {
  return {
    cart: toCartView(state.shoppingCart)
  };
}


function mapDispatchToProps(dispatch) {
  return {
    onRemoveClick: function(product){
      dispatch(removeFromCart(product));
    }
  };
}


export default connect(
  mapStateToProps,
  mapDispatchToProps
)(ShoppingCart);
```

Selectors

There are cases when we want to filter and transform the state. For this, we use pure functions called selectors that take the state as a parameter and return a new value after the transformation. We can put them in the same file as the reducer function working with the same state.

Below is the `toCartView()` selector that takes the `shoppingMap` and returns a list of all products and the total price.

```
function toCartView(shoppingMap) {
  const shoppingList = Array.from(shoppingMap.values());
  return Object.freeze({
    list: shoppingList,
    total: shoppingList.reduce(addPrice, 0)
  });
}

function addPrice(totalPrice, line) {
  return totalPrice + line.price * line.quantity;
}

export { toCartView };
```

Data Flow

Let's look at the data flow for reads and writes.

Reads from store

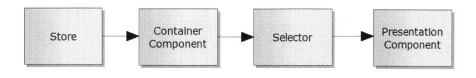

Writes to store

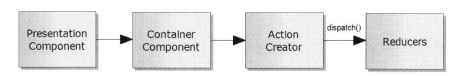

Reducers by Convention

I would like to get rid of the switch statement in the reducer function.
Functions should be small and do one thing.

Let's split the reducer into small pure functions with names matching the
action types. I will call these setter functions. Each of them takes the
state and an action as parameters and returns the new state.

```
import { Map } from "immutable";

function add_to_cart(shoppingMap, {product}) {
  const newProduct =
    incrementProductQuantity(shoppingMap, product);
  return shoppingMap.set(product.id, newProduct);
}

function remove_from_cart(shoppingMap, {product}) {
  return shoppingMap.remove(product.id);
}
```

We need to combine all these small functions together to create the original
reducer function. We can use the handleActions() utility function from
the redux-actions library for this.

```
import { handleActions } from "redux-actions";
import { Map } from "immutable";

export default handleActions(
  { add_to_cart, remove_from_cart },
  Map()
);
```

The setter functions will run by convention. When an action with type
"add_to_cart" comes in, the add_to_cart() setter function is executed.

To install redux-actions run the following command:

```
npm install redux-actions --save
```

Final Thoughts

Redux is a state manager working with pure functions.

A reducer is a pure function that takes state and an action and returns the new state.

The reducer function can be created by convention from smaller pure functions.

An action creator is a pure function that returns a plain action object.

Chapter 11: Fetching Data and MobX

In most cases, we need to get data from a Web API and display it on the screen. Let's do just that.

A simple way to do it is to create a list of products in a `.json` file. The `products.json` file stays in the `public` folder:

```json
[{
  "id" : 1,
  "name" : "mango",
  "price" : 10
},
{
  "id" : 2,
  "name" : "apple",
  "price": 5
}]
```

The `fetch()` built-in function can be used to fetch resources across the network. `fetch()` is an asynchronous function that returns a promise.

A promise is an object that represents a possible future result of an asynchronous operation.

API Utils

It is better to separate responsibilities and encapsulate the network calls in their own files. Functions doing network calls are impure.

`fetchProducts()` gets all products from the resource.

```
function toJson(response){
  return response.json();
}

function fetchProducts(){
  return fetch("/products.json")
        .then(toJson);
}

export default { fetchProducts };
```

Product Store

MobX offers an object-oriented way of working with the state.

The store is responsible for managing state but also to keep it in sync with the server.

The store keeps an observable array of products. It delegates the network calls to the api object and then updates its internal state.

```
import { observable, action } from "mobx";

export default function ProductStore(api){
  const products = observable([]);

  const fetchProducts = action(function(){
    return api.fetchProducts()
            .then(resetProducts);
  });

  function resetProducts(newProducts){
    products.replace(newProducts);
  }

  function getProducts(){
    return products.toJS();
  }

  return Object.freeze({
    getProducts,
    fetchProducts
```

```
    });
}
```

Notice that we separate use from construction, and take the `api` object dependency as a parameter in `ProductStore`.

ProductsList Container

The container component turns the `ProductList` component into an observer. When products change in the store, the `ProductList` component re-renders.

```
import { inject, observer } from "mobx-react";

import ProductList from '../ProductList';

const withPropsMapped = inject(function(stores){
  return {
    products : stores.productStore.getProducts(),
    onAddClick : stores.shoppingStore.addToCart
  };
});

export default withPropsMapped(observer(ProductList));
```

Layers

This approach leads to a layered architecture:

- The View Layer is responsible for displaying data on the page, and for handling user interactions. The View Layer is made up of components.
- The Business Layer is made of stores.
- The API Access Layers contains the objects communicating with the Web API.

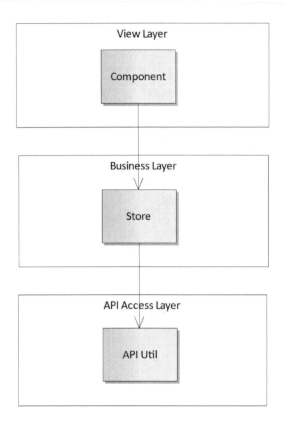

The layered architecture offers a better separation of concerns.

Entry Point

The entry point `index.js` creates the two stores passing the `api` object as a dependency, and then sends all stores to components using the `Provider`.

```
import React from "react";
import ReactDOM from "react-dom";
import App from "./App";
import { Provider } from "mobx-react";

import api from "./api/productsAPI";
import ProductStore from "./stores/ProductStore";
import ShoppingCartStore from "./stores/ShoppingCartStore";

const shoppingStore = ShoppingCartStore();
const productStore = ProductStore(api);
```

```
const stores = {
  productStore,
  shoppingStore
};

ReactDOM.render(<Provider {...stores}><App /></Provider>,
  document.getElementById("root"));

productStore.fetchProducts();
```

Final Thoughts

It is a good practice to encapsulate network calls in their own files.

MobX takes an object-oriented way of working with the state. Stores are responsible for managing the state and keep it in sync with the server.

To make things flexible and easier test we separate use from construction. For this reason, we can create all objects in the entry point file.

Chapter 12: Fetching Data and Redux Thunks

Functions doing network calls are impure. For working with impure code in Redux we need to introduce a new concept.

Asynchronous Action Creators

The action creators we have already defined are only for modifying the state in the store, nothing else.

We intend to use the `fetchProducts()` function to take all products from the network and display them on the page.

Redux architecture is a data-driven one. In order to display new products on the page, we need to update the products in the store and that will trigger a re-render of the `ProductList` component.

First, we should create the action creator for resetting all products with the new ones.

```
function resetProducts(products) {
    return {
        type: "reset_products",
        products
    };
}


export { resetProducts };
```

We first make the network call to take the products and then update the store by dispatching an action with the new products. We can do this orchestration logic using the middleware asynchronous action creators.

The following function is an asynchronous action creator:

```
import api from "../api/productsAPI";
import { resetProducts } from "../actions/productsActions";

function fetchProducts() {
  return function(dispatch) {
    api.fetchProducts().then(data =>
      dispatch(resetProducts(data))
    );
  };
}

export { fetchProducts };
```

Asynchronous action creators are functions that return other functions. The returned functions are called "thunks".

To enable them we need the **redux-thunks** library.

```
npm install redux-thunk --save
```

Reducers

A new reducer that updates the previous products with the new products is required.

```
import { handleActions } from "redux-actions";
import { List } from "immutable";

export default handleActions(
    { reset_products },
    List()
);

function reset_products(products, action) {
    return List(action.products);
}
```

combineReducers() should be updated with the new products() reducer.

```
import { combineReducers } from "redux";
import shoppingCart from "./shoppingCart";
import products from "./products";
```

```
export default combineReducers({
    shoppingCart,
    products
});
```

Entry Point

The middleware library that intercepts the dispatch and runs the asynchronous actions should be enabled when creating the Redux store.

```
const store = createStore(rootReducer, applyMiddleware(thunk));
```

Here is the full index.js file:

```
import React from "react";
import ReactDOM from "react-dom";
import { createStore, applyMiddleware } from "redux";
import { Provider } from "react-redux";
import thunk from "redux-thunk";

import App from "./App";
import rootReducer from "./reducers";
import { fetchProducts } from "./async/productsThunks";

const store = createStore(rootReducer, applyMiddleware(thunk));
store.dispatch(fetchProducts());

ReactDOM.render(<Provider store={store}><App /></Provider>,
    document.getElementById("root"));
```

Data Flow

After adding the asynchronous actions, the data flow changes:

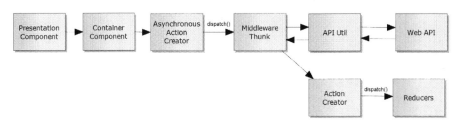

Some examples of asynchronous tasks are: network calls, timers calls.

Final Thoughts

With Redux Thunks there are two kinds of actions in an application, plain data actions and function actions. Dispatching a plain data action changes the store. Dispatching a function action does the asynchronous task and dispatches the plain object(s).

Action creators are functions that return plain objects.

Asynchronous action creators are functions that return functions. The returned functions are called thunks.

A middleware is an extension to the Redux store. It allows doing tasks after dispatching an action but before reaching the reducer. The middleware is the place for doing asynchronous tasks.

Chapter 13: Form Components with React Hooks

Form components are different than other components used for rendering the user interface because they have state.

Form elements like input, textarea and select usually have their own state and update it based on user input.

An input element with both the value and the onChange properties controlled by React is a "controlled component". The value property displays the state. The onChange event is used to modify the state.

input, textarea and select all have the value and the onChange properties.

ProductSearch Component

ProductSearch is a form component. It lets the user write the search criteria and builds the search query.

```
import React, { useState } from "react";
import "./ProductSearch.css";

export default function ProductSearch({onSearch}) {
 const [query, setQuery] = useState({text: ""});

 function updateQuery(e){
    const query = Object.freeze({ text: e.target.value });
    setQuery(query);
```

```
}

function triggerSearch(e){
    e.preventDefault();
    onSearch(query);
}

return (
  <form className="search-form" onSubmit={triggerSearch}>
  <input
    value={query.text}
    onChange={updateQuery}
    placeholder="Product"
    type="text"
    name="text"
    />
  <button type="search" className = "search-button"
    onClick={triggerSearch}>
    Search
  </button>
  </form>
  );
}
```

The ProductSearch component exposes the onSearch event property.

App Component

Once we have the query with all criteria we can filter the product list.

ProductSearch builds the search query. App listens for the search click and uses the search query to filter the products. It then sends the new filtered list to the ProducList. App is a container component.

Notice that the products parameter keeping all products is not modified.

```
import React from "react";
import { useState, useEffect } from "react";
import "./App.css";

import Header from "./Header";
import ProductSearch from "./ProductSearch";
import ShoppingCart from "./ShoppingCart";
```

```
import ProductList from "./ProductList";

//pure functions
function isInQuery(query){
  return function(product){
    return product.name.includes(query.text);
  };
}

export default function App({products, shoppingCartStore}) {
  const [cart, setCart] = useState({list: []});
  const [filteredProducts, setProducts] = useState(products);

  useEffect(subscribeToStore, []);

  function subscribeToStore() {
    shoppingCartStore.onChange(reload);

    return function cleanup(){
      shoppingCartStore.offChange();
    };
  }

  function reload() {
    const cart = shoppingCartStore.get();
    setCart(cart);
  }

  function searchProducts(query){
    const filteredProducts = products.filter(isInQuery(query));
    setProducts(filteredProducts);
  }

  return (
    <div>
      <Header />
      <div className="content">
        <div>
          <ProductSearch onSearch={searchProducts} />
          <ProductList products={filteredProducts}
```

```
            onAddClick={shoppingCartStore.addToCart}>
          </ProductList>
        </div>
        <ShoppingCart cart={cart}
          onRemoveClick={shoppingCartStore.removeFromCart}>
        </ShoppingCart>
      </div>
    </div>
  );
}
```

Final Thoughts

Form components typically have an internal state.

Form components can be created as stateful function components with React Hooks.

An input form element with the **value** and **onChange** properties controlled by React is a "controlled component".

Chapter 14: UI State with MobX

State can contain data from the Web API and data related only to the user interface.

UI Store

The UIStore keeps state related to the user interface. It is a simple store in the sense it just updates the state and triggers reactions.

In our case, the UIStore keeps the query criteria. The query is not something we want to save on the server, it is just the information we need to filter the results on the page.

Here is the UIStore:

```
import { observable, action } from "mobx";

export default function UIStore(){
  const state = observable({
    query : {
      text : ""
    }
  });

  function getQuery(){
    return state.query;
  }

  const setQuery = action(function(query){
    state.query = query;
```

```
  });

  return Object.freeze({
    getQuery,
    setQuery
  });
}
```

The UIStore is simple. It just gets and sets the query.

ProductSearch Container

Once the uiStore is created, we need to make it available to the
ProductSearch component. A new container component makes this
connection. It uses uiStore.setQuery() to handle the onSearch event.

```
import { inject } from "mobx-react";
import ProductSearch from '../ProductSearch';

const withPropsMapped = inject(function(stores){
  return {
    onSearch: stores.uiStore.setQuery
  };
});

export default withPropsMapped(ProductSearch);
```

ProductList Container

The ProductListContainer has already transformed ProductList in an
observer. We just need to make it filter the products by the query criteria.
This is accomplished by the filterProducts() pure function.

```
import { inject, observer } from "mobx-react";
import ProductList from '../ProductList';

const withPropsMapped = inject(function(stores){
  return {
    products : filterProducts(stores.productStore.getProducts(),
               stores.uiStore.getQuery()),
    onAddClick : stores.shoppingStore.addToCart
  };
```

```
});

function filterProducts(products, query){
  return products.filter(isInQuery(query));
}

function isInQuery(query){
  return function(product){
    return product.name.includes(query.text);
  };
}

export default withPropsMapped(observer(ProductList));
```

Entry Point

In `index.js` all stores, including `uiStore`, are created and then passed to components.

```
import React from "react";
import ReactDOM from "react-dom";
import App from "./App";
import { Provider } from "mobx-react";

import api from "./api/productsAPI";
import ProductStore from "./stores/ProductStore";
import ShoppingCartStore from "./stores/ShoppingCartStore";
import UIStore from "./stores/UIStore";

const shoppingStore = ShoppingCartStore();
const productStore = ProductStore(api);
const uiStore = UIStore();
const stores = {
    productStore,
    shoppingStore,
    uiStore
};

ReactDOM.render(<Provider {...stores}>
                <App />
                </Provider>,
```

```
        document.getElementById("root"));
```

```
productStore.fetchProducts();
```

Final Thoughts

Stores keep data from the backend and data related to the user interface.

The UI Store is a simple store. When state changes in the UI Store the components using it will re-render.

Chapter 15: UI State with Redux

Searching products by different criteria with Redux involves creating a new reducer that keeps the query criteria.

UI Reducer

We will create the ui reducer.

```
import { handleActions } from "redux-actions";

export default handleActions(
  { set_query },
  {
    query : { text: ""}
  }
);

function set_query(state, action) {
  return {
    ...state,
    query : action.query
  };
}
```

The ui reducer should be added to `combineReducers()`.

```
import { combineReducers } from "redux";
import shoppingCart from "./shoppingCart";
import products from "./products";
import ui from "./ui";
```

```
export default combineReducers({
  shoppingCart,
  products,
  ui
});
```

Action Creator

We need a new action to update the query. Here is the action creator for
it:

```
function setQuery(query) {
  return {
    type: "set_query",
    query
  };
}
```

```
export { setQuery };
```

ProductSearch Container

The ProductSearch component doesn't change, it remains the same.
What does change is the way it is connected to the environment.

We will create a new container component that updates the store on the
onSearch event.

When the Search button is clicked, the "set_query" action is dispatched.

```
import { connect } from "react-redux";
import { setQuery } from "../actions/queryActions";
import ProductSearch from "../ProductSearch";

function mapStateToProps(state) {
  return {
    query: state.search
  };
}

function mapDispatchToProps(dispatch) {
  return {
```

```
    onSearch: function(query){
      dispatch(setQuery(query));
    }
  };
}


export default connect(
  mapStateToProps,
  mapDispatchToProps
)(ProductSearch);
```

ProductList Container

The `ProductList` container listens to store changes. When the `query` in the store changes, the `ProductList` re-renders. `filterProducts()` takes the products from the store and filters them using the search `query`.

```
import { connect } from "react-redux";
import { addToCart } from "../actions/shoppingCartActions";
import ProductList from "../ProductList";

function mapStateToProps(state) {
  return {
    products: filterProducts(state.products, state.query)
  };
}


function mapDispatchToProps(dispatch) {
  return {
    onAddClick: function(product){
      dispatch(addToCart(product));
    }
  };
}


function filterProducts(products, query){
  return products.filter(isInQuery(query));
}


function isInQuery(query){
  return function(product){
```

```
    return product.name.includes(query.text);
  };
}

export default connect(
  mapStateToProps,
  mapDispatchToProps
)(ProductList);
```

Final Thoughts

UI state can be stored and changed in the Redux store the same way other data is stored and changed.

The UI reducer is usually a simple one.

Chapter 16: Testing

Unit tests can identify bugs and confirm that functions work as expected.

We are going to make a few tests using Jest. All test files should be named with the .test.js suffix.

The npm test command executes the tests.

Testing Redux Reducers

The next test checks that the product reducer resets all products in the store when the "reset_products" action is dispatched.

```
import { resetProducts } from "../actions/productsActions";
import productsReducer from "./products";

test("products() can reset all products", function() {
  //arrange
  const products = [];
  const newProducts = [
    {id:1, title: "apple", price: 10},
    {id:2, title: "mango", price: 5}
  ];

  //act
  const resetProductsAction = resetProducts(newProducts);
  const result =
    productsReducer(products, resetProductsAction);

  //assert
  expect(Array.from(result)).toEqual(newProducts);
});
```

We assert our expectations using the expect() function. expect() returns an "expectation" object.

The toEqual() method can be called on the "expectation" object to test the value for equality. toEqual() recursively checks every field of an object or array.

The following tests verify that the shoppingCart reducer can add products to cart, increment the quantity of an existing product and remove a product from cart.

```
import { Map } from "immutable";
import { addToCart, removeFromCart }
  from "../actions/shoppingCartActions";
import { toCartView } from "./shoppingCart";
import shoppingCartReducer from "./shoppingCart";

test("shoppingCart() can add products", function() {
  //arrange
  const cartMap = Map();

  //act
  const addToCartAction =
    addToCart({id:1, title: "apple", price: 10});
  const newCartMap =
    shoppingCartReducer(cartMap, addToCartAction);

  //assert
  const cart = toCartView(newCartMap);
  expect(cart.list.length).toEqual(1);
});

test("shoppingCart() can increment quantity", function() {
  //arrange
  let cartMap = Map();
  cartMap = shoppingCartReducer(cartMap,
    addToCart({id:1, title: "apple", price: 10}));
  cartMap = shoppingCartReducer(cartMap,
    addToCart({id:2, title: "mango", price: 5}));

  //act
  const addToCartAction =
```

```
    addToCart({id:1, title: "apple", price: 10});
  const newCartMap =
    shoppingCartReducer(cartMap, addToCartAction);

  //assert
  const cart = toCartView(newCartMap);
  expect(cart.list.length).toEqual(2);
  expect(cart.list[0].quantity).toEqual(2);
});

test("shoppingCart() can remove product", function() {
  //arrange
  let cartMap = Map();
  cartMap = shoppingCartReducer(cartMap,
    addToCart({id:1, title: "apple", price: 10}));
  cartMap = shoppingCartReducer(cartMap,
    addToCart({id:2, title: "mango", price: 5}));

  //act
  const removeFromCartAction =
    removeFromCart({id:1, title: "apple", price: 10});
  const newCartMap =
    shoppingCartReducer(cartMap, removeFromCartAction);

  //assert
  const cart = toCartView(newCartMap);
  expect(cart.list.length).toEqual(1);
  expect(cart.list[0].id).toEqual(2);
});
```

The ui reducer should be able to reset the query when the "set_query" action is dispatched.

```
import { setQuery } from "../actions/queryActions";
import uiReducer from "./ui";

test("ui() can set query", function() {
  //arrange
  const query = { text: "" };
  const newQuery = { text : "apple"};
```

```
//act
const queryAction = setQuery(newQuery);
const ui = uiReducer(newQuery, queryAction);

//assert
expect(ui.query).toEqual(newQuery);
});
```

Testing Selectors

The following test verifies that toCartView() is able to transform the
map with all products in a cart object with all products and the total
price.

```
import { Map } from "immutable";
import { toCartView } from "./shoppingCart";
import shoppingCartReducer from "./shoppingCart";

test("toCartView() can compute total price", function() {
  //arrange
  let cartMap = Map();
  cartMap = shoppingCartReducer(cartMap,
    addToCart({id:1, title: "apple", price: 10}));
  cartMap = shoppingCartReducer(cartMap,
    addToCart({id:2, title: "mango", price: 5}));

  //act
  const cart = toCartView(cartMap);

  //assert
  expect(cart.total).toEqual(15);
});
```

Testing MobX Stores

Below are a few tests for the ShoppingCartStore.

```
import ShoppingCartStore from "./ShoppingCartStore";

test("ShoppingCartStore can add products", function() {
  //arrange
  const store = ShoppingCartStore();
```

```
  //act
  store.addToCart({id:1, title: "apple", price: 10});
  store.addToCart({id:2, title: "mango", price: 5});

  //assert
  const cart = store.toCartView();
  expect(cart.list.length).toEqual(2);
});

test("ShoppingCartStore can increment quantity", function() {
  //arrange
  const store = ShoppingCartStore();
  store.addToCart({id:1, title: "apple", price: 10});
  store.addToCart({id:2, title: "mango", price: 5});

  //act
  store.addToCart({id:1, title: "apple", price: 10});

  //assert
  const cart = store.toCartView();
  expect(cart.list.length).toEqual(2);
  expect(cart.list[0].quantity).toEqual(2);
});
```

Testing a store with a dependency requires to create a fake object and pass it as the dependency.

```
import ProductStore from "./ProductStore";

test("ProductStore can reset all products", function() {
  //arrange
  const newProducts = [
    {id:1, title: "apple", price: 10},
    {id:2, title: "mango", price: 5}
  ];
  const apiFake = {
    fetchProducts : function(){
      return Promise.resolve(newProducts);
    }
  };
```

```
const store = ProductStore(apiFake);

//act
return store.fetchProducts(newProducts)
  .then(function assert(){
    //assert
    const products = store.getProducts();
    expect(products.length).toEqual(2);
  });
});
```

`Promise.resolve(value)` returns a promise resolved with the specified value.

When testing an asynchronous code that returns a promise, we need to return the promise from the test. This way Jest waits for that promise to resolve. If we don't return the promise, the test will complete before the promise is resolved or rejected and the test will not execute the assert callback.

Testing Application Start

We can create a smoke test to verify that the application can render the root component without errors.

```
import React from 'react';
import ReactDOM from 'react-dom';
import { createStore, applyMiddleware } from "redux";
import { Provider } from "react-redux";
import thunk from "redux-thunk";

import App from './App';
import rootReducer from "./reducers";
import { fetchProducts } from "./async/productsThunks";

it('App can start app without crashing', () => {
  const rootDiv = document.createElement('div');

  const store = createStore(rootReducer,
    applyMiddleware(thunk));
  store.dispatch(fetchProducts());
```

```
  ReactDOM.render(<Provider store={store}>
    <App /></Provider>, rootDiv);
});
```

Final Thoughts

Selectors and reducers are pure functions and we can create tests verifying the expected output for specific input.

Stores can be tested in isolation using fake dependencies.

A simple test rendering the root component can check if the application can start without errors.

Chapter 17: Architecture in React

Props and State

Data can take two forms, props and state.

Props

Function components take a single object argument, called "props", with all the JSX attributes.

There are two kinds of values passed as props, plain data objects and function callbacks.

State

State is data that is stored and can be changed.

State can change, but props cannot.

Local and External State

State can be local to the component and is called local state. In this case the local data can be sent to other components using props.

With Reach Hooks we can create function components with local state, using the `useState()` hook.

State can be external. It can be stored in a single store, like the Redux store, or in multiple stores, like the ones created with MobX.

The external state can be shared by multiple components.

With React Hooks we kept data as local state inside the `App` and `ProductSearch` components.

With MobX we split the state between three stores: `ShoppingCartStore`, `ProductStore`, `UIStore`.

With Redux we split the state management between three reducers: `shoppingCart`, `products` and `ui`.

Domain and UI State

The data we want to store can come either from an external Web API or from the user interface.

Domain state is taken from the backend.

UI state, or view state, is used in the user interface. It is not taken or stored on the backend.

The list of products in our case is the domain state. The shopping cart is domain state as it needs to be stored on the backend. The query search criteria are UI state.

Presentation Components

Presentation components take only plain data objects and callbacks as props.

Presentation components can have a local UI state. For example a component displaying data on multiple tabs can keep the currently selected tab as local UI state and still be a presentation component.

Presentation components are responsible for rendering the UI. Here are things presentation components don't do:

- They don't make network calls.
- They don't have access to stores.
- They don't dispatch actions.
- They don't use objects with a publish-subscribe public interface.

We can best express presentation components as pure functions with no local state.

Presentation component encourage reusable and encapsulated code.

Presentation components transform data into a visual user interface and define the callbacks to run in response to the user interactions.

Container Components

Container components are connected to the external environment and can have side effects.

Container components can read data from stores and dispatch actions.

We can use higher-order components to create containers.

UI Decomposition

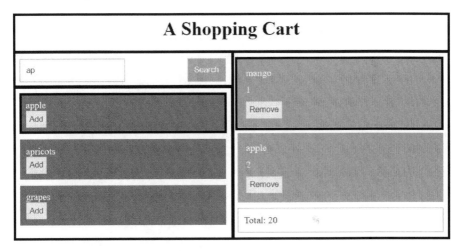

The complexity of a large UI can be handled by decomposing it into smaller pieces. Components are the basic unit for splitting the page into small parts easier to manage and reuse.

The process of decomposition is about assigning responsibilities and giving names. This makes it easy to talk and reason about.

We decomposed the page into the following components:

- **App** the root component
- **Header** a pure function rendering the header information
- **ProductList** a pure function rendering the list of products
- **ProductItem** a pure function rendering one product from the list
- **ProductListContainer** a container component displaying the products using the **ProductList** component and communicating with the store(s)

- **ShoppingCart** a pure function rendering the shopping cart
- **ShoppingItem** a pure function rendering one product from the shopping cart
- **ShoppingCartContainer** a container component displaying the cart using the **ShoppingCart** component and communicating with the store(s)
- **ProductSearch** a presentation component rendering the search form and building the search query
- **ProductSearchContainer** a container component displaying the search form using the **ProductSearch** and updating the store with the search query

Components are organized in a tree structure. In our example, we created a tree with three levels. Let's visualize it.

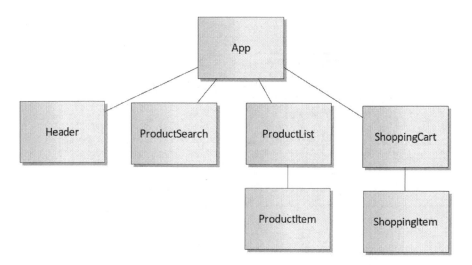

It is important to note that **ProductSearch**, **ProductList**, and **ShoppingCart** are the container components created from the presentation components with the same name.

UI as Function of State

In a sense, React allows treating the UI as a function of state. There is an equation describing this relation:

```
UI = f(state)
```

f is a mapping function that transforms data into a UI.

Note that this equation takes into consideration only the data props. The UI is not only about creating a visual representation of data but also about handling user interactions. The user interactions can be expressed using the concept of actions. Actions change state.

Unidirectional Data Flow

Views do not modify the data they received.

Views subscribe to store changes, so when the state changes views are notified to re-render. Views trigger actions on user interaction. These actions change the state. When the state is changed the associated views are re-render.

This data flow is known as the unidirectional data flow.

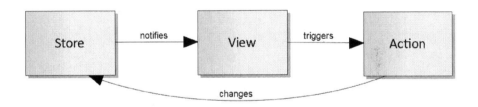

MobX Architecture

With MobX we tend to split the application into three layers:

- Presentation Layer: Presentation and Container Components
- Business Layer: Domain Stores and UI Stores
- API Access Layer: API Utils

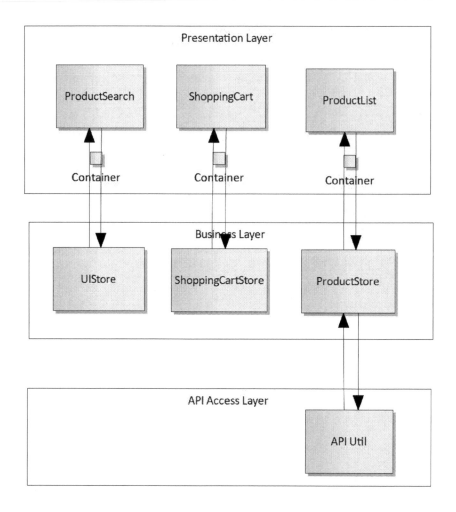

Containers make presentation components observers of stores. When state changes in a store the presentation component using that data will re-render. Container components handle the presentation components events by calling methods on stores.

When in the entry point file `index.js` the `productStore.fetchProducts()` method is called, the store delegates the network call to the `api` object. When the response gets back, the state is updated and that makes its observer components to re-render.

Redux Architecture

In a Redux Architecture we split the application into the following parts :

- Presentation and Container Components
- Reducers and Selectors
- Actions and Action Creators
- Asynchronous Action Creators
- API Utils

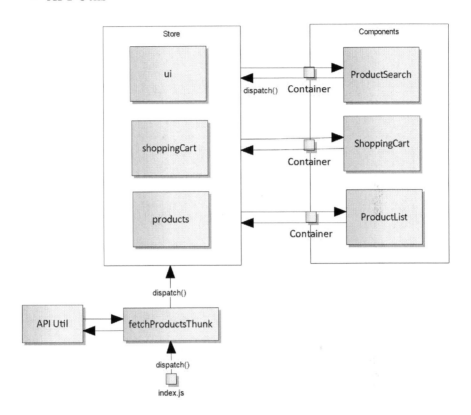

We express the UI using presentation components and aim for making them pure functions.

State management is split between reducers.

Container components are used to make the connection between the unique store and presentation components. Container components read data from the store, use selectors to transform it and send it to presentation components. Container components decide what actions to dispatch on events in the presentation components. When state changes inside the store the presentation components using that data will re-render.

The API Util objects make network calls.

Asynchronous action creators coordinate asynchronous tasks and store updates. In our case, the entry point file `index.js` dispatches a thunk function, using `fetchProducts()`. The thunk function fetches data from the network and updates the store. Updating the store with new products triggers a re-render of the `ProductList` component.

Final Thoughts

The UI can be expressed as a tree of presentation components, where each component is a function.

State can be split and managed in small parts.

Container components connect state to presentation components.

API Utils encapsulate network calls.

Redux takes a functional way of managing state, while MobX takes a more object-oriented approach. I favor Redux for working with state in a functional style.

Chapter 18: Functional Programming in React

React embraces functional programming and that's why it is of great value to master the functional programming concepts when working in React.

Array Functional Toolbox

The basic array toolbox for working in a functions style is made of the `filter()`, `map()` and `reduce()` methods.

> `filter()` selects values from a list using a predicate function that decides what values to keep.

> `map()` transforms a list of values to another list of values using a mapping function.

> `reduce()` reduces a list of values to one value using a reducer function.

As you have already seen, they were used in reducers and selectors. We are going to use them in all data transformations.

`map()` was used in list components to transform a list of values into a visual representation.

Immutability

> An immutable value is a value that, once created, cannot be changed.

In function components, props should be treated as immutable. That's it, we never modify the values in props and consider them read-only.

Even more, the state value should be treated as being immutable. For example, in `ProductSearch` when we did a new search, we didn't modify the existing `query` object, which had to be immutable anyway, but created a new one.

The transfer objects that move around the application from one component to another should be immutable.

Basically, we have two options when working with immutable values in JavaScript. One is to freeze all objects and arrays at creation with `Object.freeze()`. The other option is to use a library like Immutable.js that provides immutable data structures.

Pure functions

A pure function is a function that given the same input always returns the same output and has no side effects.

A side effect is a change of the outside environment in any way. Even more, reading data from the outside environment that can change is a side effect.

First, we should aim to create components as pure functions. That's it, they take data as props and return the markup defining the user interface.

Pure function components are easier to read and understand.

Then we should aim at making the other functions pure. Reducers, selectors, action creators are pure functions.

Higher-order functions

A higher-order function is a function that takes another function as argument, returns a function or does both.

The asynchronous action creator is a custom higher-order function that returns a function.

```
import api from "../api/productsAPI";
import { resetProducts } from "../actions/productsActions";

function fetchProducts() {
  return function(dispatch) {
    api.fetchProducts().then(data =>
      dispatch(resetProducts(data))
```

```
  );
 };
}
```

Higher-order components

> A higher-order component is a function that takes a component
> as input and returns a new component.

Reading data from the store and dispatching events are side effects. We
can keep components pure by encapsulating side effects in higher-order
components, HoC.

MobX's `observer()` is a higher-order component. The next component
`withPropsMapped()`, created by `inject()`, is higher-order component.

```
const withPropsMapped = inject(function(stores){
  return {/*code*/};
});
```

```
export default withPropsMapped(observer(ProductList));
```

Redux's `connect()` is a higher-order component.

```
export default connect(
  mapStateToProps,
  mapDispatchToProps
)(ProductList);
```

Partial Application

> Partial application is the process of fixing a number of argu-
> ments to a function by creating another function with fewer
> arguments. The returned function is a partially applied func-
> tion.

In `ProductItem` we used partial application to create a new function with
the `product` item already applied. The new function was then set as a
callback for the `onClick` event.

```
import React from "react";
import partial from "lodash/partial";

function ProductItem({product, onAddClick}) {
```

```
  return (
    <div>
      <div>{product.name}</div>
      <div>
      <button type="button"
        onClick={partial(onAddClick, product)}>
       Add
      </button>
      </div>
    </div>
  );
}
```

Currying

> Currying transforms a function that takes multiple arguments
> into a sequence of functions where each takes one argument.

We used a manually curried function when filtering products by a query.
isInQuery() is a curried function.

When calling isInQuery() with one argument it creates a new function
taking the remaining argument. Currying can be useful when the function
receives fewer arguments than necessary, like for example when is used as
a callback.

```
function isInQuery(query){
  return function(product){
    return product.name.includes(query.text);
  };
}
```

```
function searchProducts(query){
  const filteredProducts = products.filter(isInQuery(query));
  setProducts(filteredProducts);
}
```

Promises

> A promise is an object that represents a possible future result
> of an asynchronous operation.

API Util functions encapsulate the network calls that return promises. Asynchronous action creators work with promises.

Function Composition

> Function composition is a technique of passing the output of a function as the input for another function.

When creating the `ShoppingCart` container with MobX we used function composition. `withPropsMapped()` takes as input the output of `observer()`.

```
export default withPropsMapped(observer(ShoppingCart));
```

Closures

Closure can encapsulate state. Multiple closures sharing the same private state can create encapsulated objects.

```
import { observable, action } from "mobx";

//pure functions

function ShoppingCartStore(){
  const shoppingMap = observable.map();

  function toCartView() {
    return toCartViewFromMap(shoppingMap);
  }

  //actions
  const addToCart = action(function(product){
    shoppingMap.set(product.id,
      incrementProductQuantity(shoppingMap, product));
  });

  const removeFromCart = action(function(product){
    shoppingMap.delete(product.id);
  });

  return Object.freeze({
    addToCart,
```

```
    removeFromCart,
    toCartView
  });
}
```

`ShoppingCartStore()` creates an object with private state. `addToCart()`, `removeFromCart()`, `toCartView()` are closures sharing the same private state `shoppingMap`. The `this` keyword is not used.

Final Thoughts

React makes it easy to build components with functions. Function components are cleaner and easier to read. They are not using the `this` pseudo-parameter.

The best way to achieve clarity in a React application is to write as many components as pure functions.

More than that, we should try to write as many functions as pure functions.

Immutability avoids unexpected changes that create issues hard to understand.

`filter()`, `map()`, `reduce()` make data transformations easier to read.

Partial application and currying help creating new functions with fewer arguments than the original functions. The new functions can be used as callbacks.

Higher-order components help to encapsulate impure code.

Multiple closures sharing the same private state can create flexible and encapsulated objects.

About the author

Cristian Salcescu is the author of Discover Functional JavaScript.
He is a Technical Lead passionate about front-end development and
enthusiastic about sharing ideas. He took different roles and participated
in all parts of software creation. Cristian Salcescu created training courses
and knowledge sharing groups inside organizations.

Made in the USA
Middletown, DE
28 December 2019

82100848R00066